QUICK TIPS
FOR BUSY WOMEN

Cutting Through The Confusion and Finding Clarity

QUICK TIPS
FOR BUSY WOMEN

Cutting Through The Confusion and Finding Clarity

by NICOLYA WILLIAMS, CCP.

Quick Tips for Busy Women: Cutting Through the Confusion and Finding Clarity

2018 Clarity Cove Publishing

Cover art by Michael Grigsby
Foreword by Jody Holland
For more information email: Nicolya@nicolyawilliams.com

ISBN-13: 978-1633900424

ISBN-10: 1633900428

Third Edition

For every busy woman who feels like her dreams and desires

have to be pushed to the back burner,

I want you to know that you are important,

and your dreams do matter!

~ Nicolya

*T*his book is dedicated to my Grandmother, Ramona.

She is the strongest woman I know and is a true example of love.

She is my hero.

ACKNOWLEDGMENTS

*T*hank you first and foremost to my Lord and Savior, Jesus Christ. I would be nothing without you. Thank you for choosing me to write this book and allowing me the chance to have an impact on other women. I am forever grateful.

To my beautiful daughters Kaelyn and Kamryn, you two are my entire world. You are the drive behind my motivation, and EVERYTHING I do is for you. There are so many words to say I love you, but not enough words to say how much. Just know that when it seems impossible to love you more, I do. Te amo!

To my mom Kelly, thanks for modeling strength and resilience. Thanks for all of your support. For that, I could never repay you!

To my brother Alan, you always said I was capable of more than I believed. Thanks for believing in me when I did not first believe in myself.

To my Uncle Mike, thank you for your support in my book writing process, and making all of the editing details feasible. You are simply the best.

To Jessica, my friend, I love and miss you more than words can express, RIH!

To Jody Holland, thank you for believing in me and agreeing to share your expertise.

To my family and friends, I love y'all so much! Thank you for all of the love, support, and P.U.S.H!

TABLE OF CONTENTS

FOREWORD

BY JODY HOLLAND

*J*ody Holland is a writer, a fighter, and a business ignitor. He works with entrepreneurs to help them put the spark in their eyes and the fire in their bellies to dig deep and find the will to push on.

He challenges people to be true, strong, and positive in all that they do on a moment by moment basis. In the end, none of our resumes will matter, but our actions will leave a ripple effect in our world. His specialties include business assessment, survey and evaluation design and implementation, Internet technology, and organizational and individual development programs. His "Buddy 2 Boss" program has been an incredible success with companies and their managers.

www.linkedin.com/in/jodynholland

$\mathscr{B}$usy is the new normal. That was a concept I thought about a few years back and was reminded of when I read Nicolya's book. We go through life trying to figure out what matters most, where we're going, who we're supposed to be, and how the heck we're supposed to keep up. We try diligently to reduce stress in our lives and declutter our homes, only to realize that we're often just spinning our wheels and not making any headway. I see this in the lives of my clients and my own life as well. It's not until a budding author like Nicolya Williams wakes up one day and says, "Enough!" that we figure out there is a game-plan. The game plan can't be another 12-step theory, though. It has to be an actionable process of reducing the things that are siphoning off our time, our peace, and our joy. It also has to be a simple model so as to guarantee our best chance of staying the course.

Sigmund Freud dissected the model of the mind into the id, which is the preconscious and the unconscious mind; the ego, which represents the conscious mind; and the superego, which represents our conscience. It is often the super-ego that stands over us and reprimands us for not taking action. It is that component of the mind that tells us we are not good enough, or that we have failed at what we are supposed to be doing. Although the admonishment can often feel harsh, it is a saving grace for us as it stimulates the necessary motivation to prompt change. The mind, then, is like a giant wave-pool of reality. The ego generates a wave of thought into the mind through the preconscious component of the id, and finally into the id itself. It swirls around inside, and creates or validates a belief which then ripples outward until it becomes reality.

Our beliefs create our thoughts. Our thoughts give life to our actions, and ultimately, our actions generate the outcomes we see play out in our lives. In this book, you will learn the model for creating a new wave of thought that will sweep out your old belief patterns, untangle the limitations on your life and your time, and flow more harmoniously into the life you know is possible. Your *choice*, as Nicolya maps out, opens the door to the pathway of both success and peace for each sojourner on this quest.

When we choose our path, our attitude, our thoughts, and ultimately our outcomes, we are standing up and taking hold of possibility. We are grasping our potential with both hands and not letting go. If you choose to accept the limiting belief that your circumstances dictate your reality, then you will receive just that. However, if you follow the exercises and lessons in this book and choose to believe that you have the ability to change your circumstances, then you will receive all the accompanying benefits. You will learn that life is of your making—either way.

This book will help you to realize that you do, in fact, have control over your thoughts and ultimately over your outcomes. If you embrace the learning opportunities found inside, you will find that your life will begin to take on a new shape, and like Dorothy in the land of Oz, you'll learn that you've always had control, and the means to captain your own ship have been within your reach all along.

I truly hope you enjoy this book as much as I have, and that you challenge yourself and embrace the reflection exercises. These are critical to help you realign your thoughts, reboot your habits, and take full control of what happens next in your life.

You will learn that the story of your life is being written every day with every thought you send forth. You can either choose to write the story you desire or allow your circumstances and busyness to write your story for you. It's up to you. It's your choice, so choose wisely!

INTRODUCTION

"How you do anything is how you do everything."

~ T. Harv Eker

The way people approach one aspect of their life is the same way they approach everything else within their life. When we procrastinate with work, we probably procrastinate with personal obligations as well. Every now and then, we hit a point in our life where we feel as though it is too chaotic and unorganized. Some of us get frustrated with certain aspects, such as fitness or finances, while some others may feel frustrated with their relationships, or careers. As such, it can feel overwhelming to identify how to bring about the necessary changes in our life.

Quick Tips for Busy Women, was birthed from my feelings of being overwhelmed. It felt like my busyness was taking over and truly consuming me. No matter what I tried, nothing was working and I honestly felt hopeless. When I could not handle the pressure any longer, I decided to implement real steps to get myself on the right track. Because I have been where you are, and I know you do not want to stay there, I believe it is my calling to empower you with the knowledge and skills to be productive, while taking care of yourself in the process.

Consider this, both the richest and the poorest person in the world have the exact same amount of time. The difference lies within how they choose to use their time. One of the greatest things I learned is that you must take control of your time, if you want to gain control of your life. Just like a budget, many people resist the idea of controlling time. However, the truth is, either you can tell yourself how your time should be spent, or your time will take control of your life. When you are in control, you can use your time to make choices that push you closer to your goals. All in all, time management is the best tool we have to increase our success. Without good time management, you are truly unlocking the door to failure.

There is an old Amish proverb that sums up the above concept, *"The best preparation for tomorrow is the right use of today."* Be thankful for today, because it is a wonderful time to be alive. There are so many opportunities for growth and advancement. The problem is that so many people refuse to take advantage of these things. You, my friend, are different. You have decided to make a choice, by buying this book to start making a change in your life to move forward into your greatest potential.

Have you ever heard the old saying by Lao Tzu, "*The journey of a thousand miles begins with a single step.*" In other words, the best way to tackle those overwhelming tasks in our life is by choosing to approach it one thing at a time. Think about it: If I asked you to walk seven straight miles on Friday, most of you would think that I am insane. However, if I asked you instead to walk one mile a day until Friday, that would seem a bit more reasonable. That one mile will add up though and before you know it, you will accomplish the same task but in a shorter amount of time.

The truth is, we can only take on so much, and when we overwhelm ourselves, we usually fail because of the insurmountable pressure. When getting your life back in order, it is important to tackle one thing at a time. Years ago, I told myself I wanted to write a book. Just the thought of it made me sick because it seemed like too big of a pill to swallow. Yeah, I had the knowledge. Yes of course, I wanted to share the information with every woman in the world. On the reverse side, no, I did not possess the patience to sit still for a month straight to type it all up. So instead of taking it one step at a time, I overwhelmed myself with unreasonable expectations and I gave up. I did not finish a book I was passionate about, and I almost did not accomplish this goal altogether. This was simply because I could not visualize a reasonable approach. After years of putting it off, I found a great way to accomplish this goal. I began working a little bit each day. Some days I would study my topics for an hour; other days I would write for thirty minutes, and some days I spent quiet time to reflect and process my next steps. I decided I would no longer let the feeling of being overwhelmed consume me.

I am here to tell you that this is possible for you too. I don't want you to fail at reaching any of your goals because of your approach. I don't want you to not succeed in life because of a lack of direction. I don't want you to struggle because of roadblocks. I want you to be successful and to accomplish your goals. I want you to succeed, and most importantly, I want you to impress yourself.

The concept of this book is to help you to make room in your life for the things that truly matter. Reading *Quick Tips for Busy Women,* will help you to pay attention to the time-suckers in your life and learn practical tips to eliminate time drainers such as clutter, confusion, and chaos, making time for the things that truly matter. You will learn practical techniques that you can implement in your life. These are not just ideas; rather, these are techniques that I have used both personally, as well as with my clients in order to increase their clarity. When you implement these strategies, you will unlock the door to your potential and multiply your success. Most importantly, this will allow you to grab control of your life, save you a significant amount of time, and you will be able to make time for the things that matter most!

Each chapter discusses various things that impact us as women. Take time to read through each chapter. Take a moment to journal and reflect on these areas in your life. Books like these are important as they help to encourage and motivate you, and let you know that it is safe to dream, and it is possible to live out your dreams. Knowledge plays a huge role in the growth and overall productivity of individuals. Without knowledge, you can become complacent, never having the chance to learn about ways that you can improve the lives of yourself, as well as others. So thank you for taking time to educate yourself.

Now I have one favor to ask of you. Please be patient with yourself. Getting frustrated and quitting or having a negative mindset is not going to motivate you. Recent research led by a team at the University College London[1] shows that it takes at least 21 days to create a habit. Recognize that this entire book is about creating new habits and a new you. This is not a destination it is a process and your journey begins now!

---

[1]University College London (2017, n.d) *Science of Habits*. Retrieved from the University College London Website http://www.ucl.ac.uk/healthy-habits/science-of-habits

QUICK TIPS

FOR BUSY WOMEN

Cutting Through The Confusion and Finding Clarity

CHAPTER 1: THOUGHTS

"Change your thoughts and change your world."

~ Norman Peale

There are a lot of opinions about the way in which our thoughts impact our lives. The truth is our thoughts become our beliefs. Beliefs are basically internalized thoughts. These are stories that we have told ourselves which we in turn embrace as fact. If you believe that you will fail or succeed, either way, you are right. It is all about what's in your mind. After all, your mind has enormous capabilities. I am a firm believer that we are our very own cheerleader. If you do not believe in yourself, why would anyone else believe in you?

I remember being consumed in my thoughts. I would have trouble falling asleep thinking about all the things that could go wrong. The thoughts that came into my head felt like reality, and quite often they would keep me paralyzed. Eventually, I would think those things into existence, and then justify that was the reason why I thought about it all along. The truth is what you focus on grows. So choose to focus on the positive things that you want to grow in your life.

I remember in college, I had a professor tell me that statistics was the hardest class that ever existed. On the first day of class he told us that by the third class, only half of the students would still be enrolled, and by the end, it would be less than twenty five percent. While I believed him I wanted to identify a better approach so that I did not internalize what he shared with us. I chose to affirm myself every morning saying, "I can do this", and , "I will be successful". Using these words encouraged me and because I believed the words when I said them, they became my reality. I was able to pass the class and I was successful. This was one of the greatest lessons I learned on the power of our thoughts.

The thoughts we have create our emotional state of mind. Our thoughts affect our overall health. Living in a state of worry alone can increase your likelihood of depression. Our thoughts even influence the way in which we interact with others. No matter what the situation or circumstances may be, every action we take stems from our thoughts. Thoughts become our feelings. Together, thoughts and feelings create your life.

How we perceive an event significantly impacts our experience of it. For example, if you get in the car in the morning and say, "Wow, there will be a lot of traffic today", then when you get in the car, naturally you will focus on the traffic. This then confirms what you were thinking. Similarly, you could say, "Today when I drive to work, the sun will be so pretty." When you get in the car, you will focus on the sun and it will indeed be impressive. Now you have shifted your thinking from frustrated to content.

What you focus on will grow. If you focus on everything negative, you better believe you will notice each and every negative situation. When you have thoughts that are negative, challenge that thinking. Do something different to automatically change your thinking. Jump, run, laugh, but do something that immediately changes your thought process.

Break those voices down and put them into submission to your desires. We all have experiences that take place in our life which shape us, either for better or worse. If we don't handle those unconscious thoughts, we become victim to our thoughts. Negative thinking can hold you back in so many arenas (i.e., careers and relationships). This is why it is imperative that we get a handle on our thinking. This will not be easy all of the time. The more you practice changing those thoughts, the easier it becomes. Therefore, keep practicing even if it doesn't feel like it is working. You did not create that negative thinking overnight. Let's be honest — it happened over time, even if you don't know how. Therefore, challenging that thinking will also take time. Be patient with yourself and your thinking. Also, remember that practice makes perfect.

Your circumstances will not change unless you first change your train of thought. If you focus on feeling good, this will help you to find those things in life that contribute to you feeling this way. Your happiness is in your hands, and it all begins with a thought!

Your beliefs play a major role in how you view yourself and others. Your beliefs shape who you are as a person. If you ever want to live a fulfilling life, you have to conquer your thoughts. This can only happen if you take time to truly connect with yourself and reflect on who you are and who you desire to be.

WAYS TO WORK ON CHANGING YOUR THOUGHTS

1. Each time you think something negative, immediately replace it with a positive thought.

2. Practice gratitude activities, as this will help you to look at the bright side of things and become more optimistic.

3. Write down negative thoughts and rip them up. Write down positive thoughts and post them somewhere you will see them often.

4. Recite positive sayings.

5. Be kind to both yourself and to others.

In order to truly change your thoughts, you have to flood your life and your brain with all of the good things you can think of. Think of the things in your life that you are proud of. Think of the things around you that are good. Look at your surroundings and smile. When you practice focusing on the good, it creates an attitude of gratitude.

The truth is that practicing positive thinking far outweighs the opposite. When you practice this sort of thinking, you give your brain time to relax instead of being overwhelmed or consumed in poor thoughts. You allow for yourself to be more productive.

Take time to evaluate where the negative thinking comes from. I personally dealt with being a pessimist my entire life. I always saw the glass as half empty. Yes, it was a habit, but part of it was security. I realize that seems weird, so I will explain. I always felt that if I thought of all the bad things that could happen, when they actually came true, I would be able to cope better. That was probably the most inaccurate thought process I have ever had. I was never prepared for when bad things happened, and I spent so much time being miserable just waiting for something to go wrong. I had to learn that in life, I will be let down, but if I remain optimistic, the letdown won't hurt as bad. I have now been able to search for the silver lining in each situation. I have learned to make lemonade out of lemons, and I have learned to smile when the world tells me I should cry. This attitude of positivity has gotten me through some of the worst situations you could possibly imagine.

Too often, we live in a state of worry or depression. Depression comes from thinking about our past. Worry comes from living too far in the future and being concerned about all of the "what if's". My final step is to just enjoy the moment. Take time to be present and smile. Realize all of the great things that are happening in the here and now. This very moment and this very second will NEVER be relived. Genuinely enjoy it.

F.R.E.E.

F - Flood your brain and life with good things

R - Recognize the benefit of being optimistic

E - Evaluate where the negative thinking stems from

E - Enjoy the moment

REFLECTION

What did you learn about the impact your thoughts have on your life?

_____

_____

_____

_____

_____

What are three ways you can F.R.E.E. up your thoughts?

F _____
R _____
E _____
E _____

F _____
R _____
E _____
E _____

F _____
R _____
E _____
E _____

What can you say to affirm yourself?

_____

_____

_____

CHAPTER 2: HABITS

"You will never change your life until you change something you do daily. The secret to success is found in your daily routine."

~ John C. Maxwell

Habits aren't painful until you realize that they have kept you from reaching your goals. When I was in college, I would go shopping every weekend. I remember being offered my first credit card through PNC bank and I was so excited. I promised I would only spend a little bit of money on the credit card and always pay it back. It turns out, it did not happen quite that way. I spent a little money here, and little money there. Before I knew it, I maxed out my credit card. Unfortunately, that wasn't enough to stop my spending because I had made it into a habit by then. So I went to a store to buy a shirt, and went over my card balance owing over $50 in fees for a shirt that was only $14 on the sale rack. That's when reality set in and I knew I had to break this shopping habit. I assumed it would be easy, but the truth is, breaking this habit was hard.

You see, habits are only bad if they are keeping you from being successful. In this case, my habits were tearing me down. It's important that you recognize the habits in your life that are adding to your life and the habits that are taking away from it. Take some time to reflect on this. Although this was one of my bad habits, there are areas in my life where I have had some positive habits that have produced wonderful things.

I had a woman in my church pray over me, and share with me that God wanted me to reach women all around the world. I had no idea how that was ever going to happen since I had no money to travel, but I held tight to that thought. I started to journal my experiences and share them with people in my small group at church. The women in my group were so inspired, I decided I wanted to write a book to help more women. This idea kept me inspired for some time.

The trouble set in when I realized that I had no idea how I could possibly write a book. I was so overwhelmed. I decided I would make a new habit of writing a little bit each day. Some days it would be for part of a book even though I hadn't had a topic picked out yet, the other days it would be just because. What I found was that the more I wrote, the more I enjoyed it and the more I wanted to share. What started off as an idea turned into a healthy habit. This showed me the power of having habits that serve your goals! I want to share with you ways to create habits in your life in the same manner! So here we go!

The key to being productive is to create effective processes. In order to do this, we have to be open and honest with ourselves. We did not get messy or have financial problems all because of other people. This is something that happens over time, and is most likely reflective of our habits.

The secret to success is found in your daily routine. John C. Maxwell once said, *"Show me your routines, habits and rituals and I will show you your future"*[2]. The quality of your life will always be a reflection of the quality of your routines, habits and rituals.

A SK YOURSELF:

- What do I do each day?

- What do my habits say about me?

I recommend actually tracking your habits for at least 24 hours before working through this. You could use the notepad in your phone to jot these things down. If you have a better approach to track these habits, that is fine, the intention is for you to measure and understand what you are doing, and how often. It is important to reflect on these things, because ultimately it determines your destiny!

Your life won't change unless you have insight and then you actually implement change. That begins with understanding your patterns. Next, you must practice discipline and taking control of your habits!

---

[2]Maxwell, J.C (2014, August). *John C. Maxwell: The Daily Routines of Successful Leaders.* Retrieved from Success.com Online http://www.success.com/article/john-c-maxwell-the-daily-routine-of-successful-leaders

The truth is that our habits and choices compound. If you choose to eat unhealthy for one day it doesn't really hurt, but if you do it for several weeks then the impact is huge! If you choose to drink 64 ounces of water for one day that's nice, but if you do it every day for a year then the impact it has on your health is phenomenal. This is why it is imperative that you stay on top of your habits. You want the compound effect to work in your favor! If you change your habits once in a blue moon, don't be upset when you only see the results once in a blue moon!

When we have bad habits, they can cause trouble in important areas of our lives. These habits can cause a block in the path of us trying to reach our goals. Our habits shape our lives because we are what we do consistently; this is why it is so important that we both identify and address these habits. Everything is hard before it gets easy, and this especially true of our habits. Developing habits in the beginning is challenging, but the more you practice them the easier they become and it is almost like second nature patterns.

If you have done what I recommend, you are now ready to practice visualization. Visualize what it would feel like to be productive and disciplined. What would your life look like? What would you be able to accomplish? When you visualize this, it will inspire you to work towards making your habits positive.

Now, I want you to take a moment to list each habit that you have that negatively impacts you. This could be buying fast food, smoking, scrolling through social media time lines, watching too much TV, etc. Each of our small day-to-day habits have big effects on us. We often think, "Oh, I can spend a $4 on a cup of coffee today", but before you know it, you have spent $120 at the end of the month on cups of coffee.

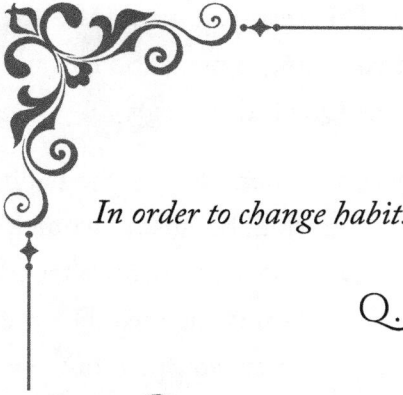

In order to change habits, I like to use a strategy I call

Q.U.I.T

Q - Quiet your mind

U - Understand your purpose

I - Implement a plan

T - Take action

Therefore, for an increased chance of success, you would use the Q.U.I.T acronym for each habit that you want to break. So let's use an example of a bad habit and apply the Q.U.I.T. strategy.

First, spend time quieting your mind, and then identify the habit that is most important to break. This is important because as women, we have many things we often want to work on, but when we try to do too much at once, we aren't successful in any one area. For the sake of having the success you desire, I ask that you pick out one habit. Don't fear; you purchased the book so you can always come back and apply this information to another habit that you want to break or add after you get a handle on the first one.

Second, let's pretend you decide that you want to break the habit of skipping your workouts. Now, you must identify the reason it is important to create this new habit. Some examples may be because your clothes are no longer fitting well, or you are unhappy with the extra weight, or it could even be that your health is in danger due to your failure to follow through with working out. It is important that you have a good reason as to why you want to create a new habit. Without a reason that speaks to you, the habit will not seem important, and you will be less likely to take those steps allowing you to be successful in creating a new habit. I call this a pain point. People are motivated by things they do not want or by some amount of pain. When you identify this area, you will push harder than if you are doing it just because someone told you it was a good idea.

The third step is to implement a plan. Some examples would be to schedule your workout and write it down so that you treat it as if it is a business meeting. We all know you would not miss those.

Another step you could take in the plan would be to find a workout buddy or an accountability partner. These are two different individuals who will help you in the steps to reach this goal. These are just a few examples of some ways that will help you put this plan into action, but remember, you're not limited. There are many ways that you can accomplish goals. Plans can include having an accountability partner, reviewing goals each day, meeting with people who can relate or simply changing daily patterns. For example, I had a client try to change her habit of spending. Part of her plan was to drive a different direction for work so she did not pass a coffee shop and feel tempted to purchase coffee. For whatever habit you are trying to break, the plan will look different.

The last step is to take action. This step is most important. Many times, people set a goal to create a new habit or erase a bad one; they set steps, but fail to take action. Taking action can be the hardest part of the entire process. It is easy to identify and understand why you want to change, but to actually change the habit is an entirely different story. Be gentle with yourself. Remember that the habit did not develop overnight, and therefore will not be changed immediately. Just stay focused and do not overdo it. We all know the saying, *"Slow and steady wins the race."* [3] So, do not expect perfection; just be steady.

There's an old quote that says, *"Vision without action is just a dream."* [4] Do not let yourself become limited, but instead begin to take those

[3]Aesop. (n.d.). BrainyQuote.com. Retrieved April 5, 2017, from BrainyQuote.com Web site: https://www.brainyquote.com/quotes/quotes/a/aesop379510.html

[4]Joel A. Barker. (n.d.). BrainyQuote.com. Retrieved April 5, 2017, from BrainyQuote.com Web site: https://www.brainyquote.com/quotes/quotes/j/joelabark158200.html

steps that will get you to your final destination. Take a post-it note and hang it up. You could write - my reason for working out is: I want to be healthy. It is imperative that we truly remember our reason why. This will give us momentum when we feel like giving up.

Q.U.I.T.

Q - Quiet your mind

U - Understand your purpose

I - Implement a plan

T - Take action

REFLECTION

What habits do I have that negatively impact me?

_____

_____

_____

_____

_____

Does this habit serve me? If so, how?

_____

_____

_____

_____

_____

How can I Q.U.I.T. this habit?

Q _____

U _____

I _____

T _____

Why is it important that I make changes today to increase my positive habits?

_____

_____

_____

_____

_____

How will I hold myself accountable through this process?

_____

_____

_____

_____

_____

"People with goals succeed because they know where they are going.
It's as simple as that."

~ Earl Nightingale

$\mathscr{I}$t was New Years 2012. I told myself this year would be different. I didn't know why or how, I just knew I wanted it to be different. I spent all of 2012 waiting for a change like it was going to fall out of the sky, and into my life. By the end of 2012 I hadn't accomplished anything. I felt defeated, discouraged and disgusted with myself. I remember telling my friend how mad I was for not accomplishing what I wanted. She asked me what was it that I had hoped to accomplish and I couldn't tell her, because I didn't know. I had failed at reaching a goal that I never set. I learned from that day forward that setting goals is like a map that directs my steps. To this day, I am addicted to setting and reviewing my goals frequently because I know without doing that, I won't ever get anywhere worth going.

I don't want you to be in the same position as I once was, wondering around waiting for success to just happen. It's time to get really clear regarding your goals. This is a chance for you to replace some of your old goals with new goals that are more powerful! In order to do that, the first step is to get clarity around what it is that you desire to accomplish. The reason that people often feel unfulfilled desires is because they are usually uncertain about what it is that they want, or they are uncertain about how to work towards what they desire. When you live in this state of mind it can impact your focus, your dedication and even your beliefs.

Have you ever reached your goals and felt depressed? Maybe because it wasn't what you thought it would be, or the goal was not clearly defined and you reached a different aspect of that particular goal. How many times have you set goals, but fallen short on taking the steps to get there? Maybe because you feel overwhelmed or discouraged? Or maybe it's because the goal did not feel important to you. Another reason could include a lack of surety on the way in which we should approach this goal. Either way, there were some complications as it relates to our goals.

Life is a process. If we had everything figured out in one day, what would the purpose of the next day be? We have to learn to respect the journey. The journey is what matters in the end. When we embrace our journey, we are able to put the purpose of our goals into perspective.

Never feel limited with your goals. You can set multiple goals for each area of your life (personal, financial, career, etc.). It is actually good to work on goals for every area because the goals will be different in each domain.

When I think of goals, I have an acronym, D.A.R.E, that I apply to my goals, which helps to increase the likelihood of me being successful with them.

The first step in D.A.R.E. is D: Dream big. I first begin with dreaming about what it is I want. I also give myself permission to dream big. I don't want to dream that I can make $25,000 a year. If I do that, then my goals will be set around that. I want to dream big because even if the goal is not met, my actions put me on the right path to eventually reach the goal I desired. Once you identify your dream, set your goal. The second step is A: Align your actions with your goal. We must recognize that our goals can only be met if we take action steps to get there.

The third step is R: Refuel your faith and focus. There are many times you may set a goal and begin to feel discouraged because it feels too overwhelming or any of the other reasons. Keep encouraging yourself, so your faith doesn't die. You can do this by looking at your progress thus far. Thinking about how far you have come often allows you to keep pushing. You could do this by putting pictures up of what life will look like when this goal has been accomplished. You could even motivate yourself by reading stories of people who worked past their comfort zone and see the good things that came from that. The truth is so many people quit because they do not realize how close they were to the finish line. I can't tell you how many times I was ready to give up when I was in college, or how many times I was uncertain about writing this book, but I am happy that I found various ways to refuel my faith while working through those tough emotions. So stop giving up.

The last step is E: Evaluate your progress. As you work to reach goals, continuously make an effort to evaluate where you are in the process of meeting your goals. It's important to do this because you want to make sure that you are not getting off track.

Learning from experience coupled with reflection has a greater impact, and is more effective. Reflection time also increases your confidence in being able to make the necessary changes. Please take time to reflect on your biggest takeaways from this chapter. What areas do you already have a good handle on? Which areas need improvement? What steps will you take beginning TODAY to make change in the direction you want to go?

Let go of goals that do not match up with your priorities, and let go of goals that are not personal. Too many times we set goals based on things that other people want for us. These goals never succeed because there is no passion involved. When you are passionate, you are dedicated and willing to work hard to achieve what you want.

In order to ensure that your goals are personalized, set them without having someone tell you what you should do. Set your goals based on your mind's desire. Your goals should make you excited. If they make you bored or sad, they are probably goals that are not personal to you.

Another thing that is helpful is to make sure you write your goals down daily. This helps to reinforce what you hope to accomplish. Writing down goals allows us to be clear about what it is we want. When we write them down daily, they serve as a reminder to take action. Taking action on goals should be a daily event, and when we write them down, we reinforce this concept. This also helps us to overcome forgetfulness or resistance. Lastly, when we write our goals down daily, we are able to track our progress. It is interesting to write them down daily because sometimes things change. This allows you to take time to reflect on what those changes may mean for you.

If it is not obvious now, I will make it clear:

- I am a big advocate for breaking things up into more manageable chunks.

- I break up my goals into small steps.

- I sometimes break my exercise into small sessions equaling a big session.

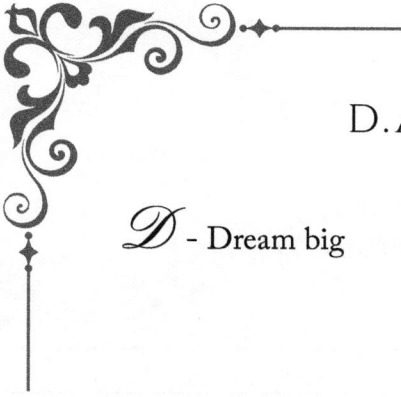

D.A.R.E.

D - Dream big

A - Align action with goal

R - Refuel your faith

E - Evaluate your progress

REFLECTION

What goals will you D.A.R.E. to set today?

D _____

A _____

R _____

E _____

How will you begin working towards this goal?

_____

_____

_____

_____

_____

What has gotten in the way of you reaching goals you have previously set?

_____

_____

_____

_____

_____

CHAPTER 4: SCHEDULE

"If you talk about it, it's a dream. If you envision it, it's possible. But if you schedule it, it's a reality."

~ Anthony Robbins

As a single mother of two daughters, a student, and a full time employee I had to learn to grab control of my schedule. Now, this wasn't always easy, but I had one situation that changed my entire perspective. I remember what happened as though it were yesterday. I had a huge group project due and kept putting it off because I just didn't feel like doing it. The night before it was due, I sat down to work on the paper portion. About five minutes into my work session, my daughter ended up having some seizure like symptoms. I was terrified. I immediately rushed her to the hospital and was there the entire night. Luckily all was well with her, and we have never experienced that again. But reality set in that I would have to come up with an excuse to my team about why I never completed my part. I remember having to tell my team - it was painful for me and they were pretty upset. I promised myself from that day forward, I would not put myself in that situation intentionally. You see accidents happen, but this was something I could have controlled had I planned ahead and stuck to my schedule. I wasted much of my time on things that did not matter, when I should have invested my time on the responsibility that I had.

How much time would you estimate that you waste each day on things that do not really matter? Between phone calls, social media, TV, small chat, and procrastination, you're probably wasting several hours each day. Some studies through Forbes Magazine show that people are wasting up to 70% of their time doing meaningless work. [5] If that doesn't bother you, I don't know what will. Time should not be looked at lightly. Life is short and we must make the most of it. Time is irreplaceable. To me, wasted time is worse than wasted money, because you can never get your time back.

Many women believe that it is impossible to get a better grasp on their time. This is not true. In fact, if you organize your schedule better, you will reduce your stress and you will be able to approach your timetable better.

We live in a busy world where we are required to take on multiple projects and responsibilities at a time. We could be in the middle

---

[5]Conner, S. (2015, July). *Wasting Time At Work: The Epidemic Continues.* Forbes Magazine Online. Retrieved from Forbes Magazine Online. https://www.forbes.com/sites/cherylsnappconner/2015/07/31/wasting-time-at-work-the-epidemic-continues/#43c4f8ec1d94

of a paper for school, completing a project for work, starting a new group at our child's school, and involved with our church. With all of the demands on our time, it can be challenging to figure out how to tackle our responsibilities appropriately.

At some point, we each get to a spot where we begin to feel overwhelmed. In order to fight against being too stressed with all of our responsibilities, we have to learn to practice managing our schedule appropriately. When you implement an effective schedule, you are better able to plan out your goals and the time you will work on them. In addition, you are able to make more time for the things that matter.

Have you ever found yourself looking at other people who seem to have so much extra time? Do you want in on the secret? Successful people all have one thing in common, and that is that they place a high value on their time. They work hard to become better organized as well as more efficient every day. It is not something that they try to implement once or twice. It is like a muscle that must be trained daily. So they implement it each day and eventually it becomes a habit, because they are aware of the great impact that valuing their time has. They avoid slipping into situations which could be viewed as a waste of time (i.e. checking emails every hour, small talk with coworkers, scrolling through social media time lines, etc). This may seem complicated to you, but you can achieve this in your life as well.

To accomplish this, I have created an acronym that will help you improve your schedule through minor tweaks. S.T.A.R.T.

stands for Stop saying yes, Take projects that matter, Allow down time, Reflect on current time-suckers and Teach yourself to prioritize.

The first thing to start our schedule off on the right foot is to stop saying yes to every single thing. We often feel like we have to say yes to please people or in order to avoid feeling guilty. This is not the case. When we say yes to everything, we are saying no to things that matter to us. This goes along with step two; when we take on projects that we enjoy or that serve us, we don't feel as stressed. This also reinforces the importance of our value.

The third step is to allow for down time. We often feel that we have to keep busy at every moment of the day. That's credit to the old adage, *"I'll sleep when I die."* Stop doing this to yourself. Overworking is the number one cause of burnout. Plus, when you give yourself time for rest, you are able to refuel yourself. This gives you a fresh and more productive start.

The fourth step, I believe is the most important. When you first want to change your schedule, take a moment to study your current daily routines and plans. Start by identifying all of the things that you do that do not serve you. This could include, "I spend two hours a week watching reality TV because I need mindless entertainment." This may not be helpful if you want to find more time with your family. On the other hand, this could be helpful for someone who is a life coach or therapist, and wants to learn about common issues we are facing in society today.

You have to remember this activity is unique to you, and what you hope to get out of a new schedule. I will share a personal example of a way that I altered my schedule. I had a really unique situation a few years ago. I was in grad school, so each day when I got off of work, I would rush home so that I could start my papers or my reading for that week. The problem was I spent an hour stuck in my car, because the time of day that I left was in the middle of rush-hour traffic. I decided that sitting in traffic was the biggest time-sucker in my entire schedule. I then changed my schedule up a bit. I stayed about thirty minutes after work ended and did some of my reading in my car, or sometimes in my office (when I did not feel like I would be distracted). This thirty-minute stay time cut off forty minutes of my travel time and I was twice as productive as before. This is something I was only able to realize by reflecting on those things that drained my time.

The last part of my handy acronym is to take time to prioritize. Each night before I go to bed, I write down all of the tasks for the next day. When you go to bed with a plan, you wake up with a purpose. Also each Sunday, it is important to plan for the week ahead. These plans allow you to have a guideline to follow, in order to ensure that you are always on the right track. When you plan, you are able to organize your tasks in the order of importance. If you have a project due at work on Tuesday, but also have to finish your taxes next Saturday, the obvious answer is that you need to work on the project first. Many people put off difficult tasks because they do not want to do them, but it often puts them in a bind when the project is due and they are out of time. Do the biggest tasks first especially when they are due soon. You will thank yourself later.

It is possible for you to turn your biggest weakness into your greatest strength. I learned that this was possible by initiating a change between both my habits and my schedule.

When working with my clients I often hear this phrase over and over again, "My life is a constant battle between wanting to sleep in but also wanting to be successful". The truth is you can only choose one or the other!

One tactic that I implemented in my schedule was what I learned through a life transformational book called *The Miracle Morning*. In this book, Hal Elrod discusses the number one success secret is to rise early. I can hear you now groaning and saying how much of a morning person you are NOT! I get it, I have been there. So to increase my morning time, I slowly rolled my clock back a little each day until now waking up at 5:00am doesn't seem so overwhelming. One of my clients waited for daylight savings time to roll her time back. Whatever works for you is great, but I highly suggest using the morning time.

Individuals who rise early are more productive, have more energy, have better control of their habits, make it a priority to take care of themselves, and are more punctual! According to Joe Duncan from Before 5am, it has been proven that between 5am-8am is the prime time for goal achievers! This is all because they are uninterrupted, more dedicated, and more focused.

Doing this frees up your schedule for later in the day to do activities that you really enjoy (i.e. park time with your children, or a movie date with your spouse). These facts should challenge every excuse you plan to throw my way of why the morning isn't good for you. Remember we have to do what is effective, not what feels good! So get rid of the excuses, wake up and work so that you can live your dream!

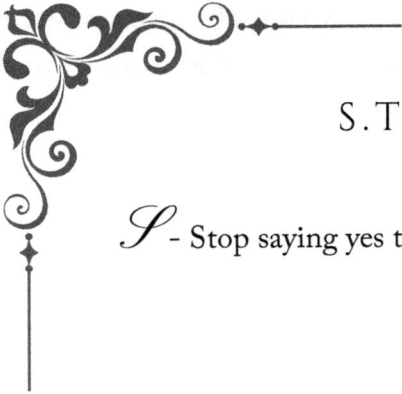

S.T.A.R.T

S - Stop saying yes to everything

T - Take projects that matter

A - Allow for down time

R - Reflect on current time-suckers

T - Teach yourself to prioritize

REFLECTION

Through this reading, what did you learn about your schedule? This could include areas needed for growth and also areas that you have done well in.

_____

_____

_____

_____

_____

What can you S.T.A.R.T. today that will help to improve your schedule?

S _____

T _____

A _____

R _____

T _____

What can you say no to today?

_____

_____

_____

_____

CHAPTER 5: HOME

"Have nothing in your house that you do not know to be useful or believe to be beautiful."

~ William Morris

Home is where the heart is. When you live in utter chaos, it will reflect in your mind and day to day choices. In 2013, I had a 4 year old and a newborn baby. I remember feeling depressed and overwhelmed. I assumed it was because I was adjusting to being a mother again. My newborn had a horrible case of colic, and I remember being up every night. This late night at the end of May was different though. For once, I decided I was going to take advantage of the extra hours since I was awake anyway. So I decided to organize and clean; I think part of me wanted to make the time fly by, while the other part of me was sick of the mess. The more I cleaned, the better

I felt. In that moment, I learned that even though your mind is cluttered, your home and environment doesn't have to be. In fact, once you start to organize or make more sense in your environment, that will reflect itself in your life.

Who loves cleaning up? Don't be the first to jump at the thought of cleaning your home. Even though I am obsessive-compulsive in regards to my cleaning habits, I do not jump at the idea of cleaning up my home. Cleaning up our area is not always something we enjoy doing, but let's be honest, it is definitely needed.

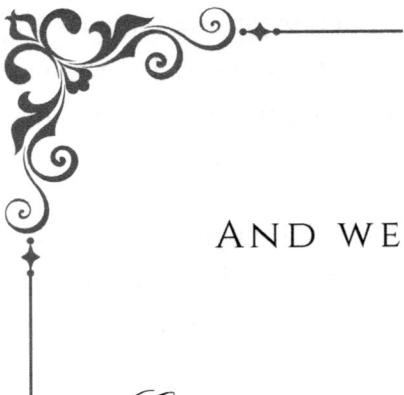

AND WE ALL C.A.N.

C - Clear out clutter

A - Alternate the way you hold on to memorable items

N - Nurture the process

We all have clutter in one way or another. You may be a magazine collector or you may have a shoe fetish. The truth is, holding on to those things is not as important as we believe it is. The first thing I recommend doing is identifying which area in your home is most cluttered. I then would reflect on the underlying issue. Identify why this clutter exists. Identify where the root of the clutter is from.

I will share a personal story. Growing up, I was always very short, and I still am. Unfortunately, my feet didn't quite match my height and they were very large. When I was in middle school, I was teased constantly about the size of my feet. I was even the brunt of jokes within my own circle of friends and amongst my own family. They would call me clown feet and everything else. I spent years stuffing my feet in shoes that were too small just so that others would not laugh at me. When I got older, I decided that I was not going to intentionally buy shoes that were too small for me. Instead, I overcompensated and bought shoes that I did not need. This was all to fill a void and to cover my insecurity. The truth is it took me thirty years to realize that I cannot change the size of my feet, nor do I want to. My feet are large, but they are strong and they are perfectly made.

I know that sounds petty now, and I agree, but I had to be real with myself in order to identify where the clutter with my shoes came from. So as I suggested previously, first dig deep to see if there is a reason behind your clutter. Do you still have all of the belongings of a deceased loved one because of the sentimental value? Are you holding on to all of your children's schoolwork and art photos because you want to save memories, or because it makes you feel guilty to throw them away? I understand these reasons, and I am sure there is good meaning behind the majority of the things we do.

Although the principal behind it all makes sense, we have to think of the impact it is having on us today. So instead of holding onto those items, look at suggestion number two and three to determine a way you can alternate your approach to making memorable items last without increasing your clutter.

The first step is to clear out clutter. In order to get started, there are a few tips that I will give you. These do not have to be done in any particular order, but they are all part of this process.

Get your family involved. When you have others helping you clean, you teach them responsibility, and it helps make the process more doable.

Take pictures of things that have value and then part ways with the item. Taking pictures allows you to still "hold on" to the item without it causing too much clutter in your home. This is an example of a way to alternate your approach to clutter.

Find a neat place for all of your children's artwork. I have a co-worker who picks her favorite pictures, laminates them and hangs them inside of her kitchen cabinets. Most people will never decorate the inside of cabinets, but this a great way to showcase work and for it not to take up too much space.

If your house is extremely cluttered, begin by tackling one room at a time. I would say go for the room that is least cluttered because once you get through that room, you will have built up the momentum and courage to continue into other areas of your house.

Here is my personal cleaning schedule:

- Monday - vacuum home, clean out old food in the fridge
- Tuesday - sweep and mop the floors
- Wednesday - clean up the bathroom(s)
- Thursday - wash and put away all of the sheets and towels
- Friday - wash and put away all of the clothes
- Saturday - tidy up things that may have gotten out of place
- Sunday - rest

Washing dishes is a chore that should be done on a daily basis, unless you have a dishwasher.

When we come home from work on Friday and we have to spend the entire weekend trying to straighten up our house, we can be overwhelmed and frustrated. It can feel like there is never any downtime. This is why I am a big advocate for breaking household chores down into smaller pieces and enjoying the majority of the day. On average, I spend about 20-30 min cleaning each day (except Sunday). This is easier to find time for instead of setting aside an entire day. When we break down cleaning routines into small chunks, it feels like it can truly be accomplished. This is what I mean by nurture the process. Recognize that it takes time to adjust it to fit your needs and your schedule. Also be patient with yourself understanding that we are all a work in progress, and this task may come easier to some than others, and that is okay.

When you begin to clean up your house, you will be able to find things that you probably have forgotten about, and you will begin to feel at ease and much happier. You won't feel as stressed or overwhelmed, and you will set an example for those around you (your children or even friends).

Four things to do once the clutter is gone:

Look at the benefits of the things you have saved. I am sure there is value to those items.

Promise yourself that you will only buy the things that are absolutely needed. When we hold off on wants, we are usually able to make room for those things that are necessary.

Get your loved ones involved. Have your kids declutter their room, or help a friend organize something in their house. Once you involve others, the activity is much more pleasurable.

Congratulate yourself. It is not easy to give up things that you felt provided you comfort. Give yourself a huge pat on the back for the progress.

I have people ask what the process for getting children involved is. I suggest making it mandatory that they clean their room at the end of EVERY day. This has countless benefits. These benefits include the fact that it teaches responsibility, it helps children realize that more isn't always better, and it allows them to sleep better in their room. In addition, it prevents accidents and it is an obvious indication that the day has ended, which in turn lets them begin tomorrow on a fresh foot. These are just a few of the benefits. You would think that with all these benefits it would be easy, but I am not going to lie to you. In the beginning, it will be a bit of a challenge, but once you make this process non-negotiable, the kids will be on board.

My friends and family always compliment me on the cleanliness of both my home and my car. This is not an easy feat. This is something that I work hard for, and make a priority. I have built a cleaning pattern into my schedule and I stick to it. In the same way that I have planned work meetings, my cleaning time is perfectly crafted into my schedule. This prevents me from feeling overwhelmed.

C.A.N.

C - Clear out clutter

A - Alternate the way you hold on to memorable items

N - Nurture the process

REFLECTION

What did you learn about your home through reading through this chapter?

_____

_____

_____

_____

_____

How do you know you C.A.N. make the needed changes in your home?

C _____

A _____

N _____

What have you been afraid to let go of and why? In what way can you alternate holding on to those valuables?

_____

_____

_____

_____

_____

What are some effective ways that you can approach your home cleaning routine?

_____

_____

_____

_____

_____

What changes can you make in your home starting today?

_____

_____

_____

_____

_____

CHAPTER 6: FINANCES

"Money is only a tool. It will take you wherever you wish, but it will not replace you as the driver."

~ Ayn Rand

I promised myself, I would be different.

I wouldn't try to fit in with what everyone else was doing, and I would never let myself get in debt like my family. I set up what I thought was a foolproof plan to keep myself from going into debt. In reality, what I made was a plan to pay my bills. That's great and all, but I never took into consideration what would happen in the case of an emergency...

We should all be preparing for one, because in reality they do come. In my situation, it did come true. My car transmission blew apart and I was looking at a $1,500.00 repair! I was sick to my stomach.

It took me three weeks to recover from this and a ton of bus rides to work. But what I learned in from this incident is that it is imperative that you plan for scenarios like this. This situation taught me the importance of saving as well. This is why I want to share tips with you to help you gain clarity regarding your finances.

So let's talk money! Finances—what fun! Literally, I want to make your finances F.U.N. I use this acronym when I am working with clients regarding finances. F stands for free up any unnecessary expenses. U stands for understanding the importance of getting in control of your money. N is for noticing your spending habits. Everyone likes to think of money as bad or stressful. Money is only stressful when you are not in control of it. I am a firm believer that you must tell money how to be spent, not the other way around. When you become consumed in things or keeping up with other people, money will always be a sore subject for you. Instead, focus on building and growing your income. This happens through daily discipline and having a mindset that is focused on your goals. If your goals are to buy a new house and you are focused on that goal, you are less likely to spend money on takeout every single day of the week. This is why keeping your goals in the front of your mind at all times will positively impact your lifestyle.

Finances can be such a taboo topic for many. I hate that more people do not talk about finances and the role it plays in our life. We are taught to keep our money life private and to keep up with the Joneses publicly! That's such an oxymoron, and quite frankly it's ridiculous. This way of living isn't doing anything other than hurting us.

Having cluttered or chaotic finances isn't always visible in the same way that you may think of clutter. You may also think that you can avoid cluttered finances because it isn't always apparent when you avoid checking your financial status, but the truth is it will always catch up with you. Take time to reflect on your budget. For the next week, write down everything that you spend money on. Then identify what was a need, and what was a want. Also identify what things you are enrolled in or buying that you no longer need. These are called unnecessary expenses. This could be that you purchased a Netflix account and now you do not even remember your login. That is an unnecessary expense, and when you add up all of the months you paid for without even accessing the service, you have basically thrown away money. I don't care how much you make a year; no one should be throwing away money.

I had a lovely friend who was living lavishly. She traveled with her spouse, bought every new purse possible, and even had a BMW. She was in debt, but usually paid the minimum balance and missed some payments here and there, but she was living the free life so she didn't see a reason to make changes. She did not realize the weight that she was carrying until it was too late. She recently decided that she wanted to get a loan for a purchase of a home. When it came time to applying for the loan, she was denied. She could not buy a house, and the worst part of it all was that she did not have a single dollar saved in her retirement. While having things is fun for the moment, what happens when you can't get the things you NEED? Or what happens when you are older and ready to retire, but have nothing to your name? There are real consequences to not being on top of your finances. This is why it is important to understand the impact that finances have on our lives.

This is the final and last step. This step is noticing what is getting in the way of you being on top of your finances. So ask yourself, what is it that hinders you from working on your financial well-being? Is it that you want nice things? Is it your friends who always convince you to travel with them? Is it your co-workers asking you to join for happy hour every day? Is it buying Starbucks on your way to work?

The truth is we can only change bad habits if we identify the root of where they began. I know for me personally, I worked full time, attended school and raised two young kids. I was a very busy mom! I spent most of my money on fast food because there never seemed to be enough time in one day, especially when it came time for grocery shopping or cooking.

When you stop spending money, you will want to find something to replace that empty space with. Without filling that void, you can easily fall victim to your old habits again. When you are tempted to log online to shop, find a motivational blog or an educational blog in the meantime. Instead of going to happy hour every week, maybe spend that time going on a walk to fill time.

Since I have begun to manage my money better, I personally like to donate when I can. This helps me feel fulfilled knowing that I helped someone else in his or her time of need. This has a greater impact than when I buy my third black purse for the year. When you clean up your money habits, you make room for your money to be used on things that truly matter to you and have a lasting impact. Changing your financial habits is a very challenging task. Better financial planning is worth it in the long run.

Ten things you should stop spending money on:

1. Fast food. Start to meal prep and on days when you're in a rush, you will have something ready.

2. Starbucks (yes I know you hate me for this). The truth is most people love coffee but it does not have to be bought every day. Challenge yourself and make it at home a few days a week.

3. CDs or movies. Choose a subscription service instead of buying a new CD or movie each time they come out. Try using Apple Music for songs or Netflix for movies.

4. Bottled water. You can buy a filter and fill up a water bottle. This will save you tons.

5. Vending machine snacks. These snacks are always way over-priced! We all have cravings, so be sure to put some snacks in your office.

6. Gas station items. Many people think it's convenient to get needs here while filling up your tank, but they are way overpriced.

7. Nail polish. No woman in the history of womanhood died because of a lack of nail polish choices.

8. Brand name products. Many off-brand items are better than the brand name products, and they are always cheaper.

9. Cable. There are so many streaming services available for a fraction of the cost of cable. Plus, you won't have to pay for

a bunch of unwatched TV channels. Also try to spend time reading instead of sitting in front of the TV.

10. In-game purchases. Many people are playing app games such as Candy Crush. Do not waste your money on the extra purchases. Even though it is only one or two dollars, that definitely adds up.

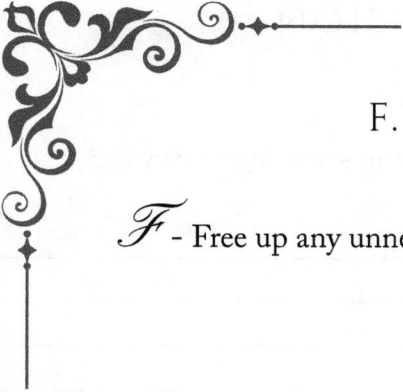

F. U. N.

F - Free up any unnecessary expenses

U - Understand the importance of getting control of your money

N - Notice your personal spending habits

REFLECTION

What are some things you need to stop spending money on?

_____

_____

_____

_____

Why is being financially sound important to you?

_____

_____

_____

_____

What steps will you take today to reach your financial goals?

_____

_____

_____

_____

How can you make handling finances F.U.N.?

F _____

U _____

N _____

CHAPTER 7: HEALTH

"Health is like money; we never have a true idea of its value until we lose it."

~Josh Billings

$\mathscr{I}$ had just turned thirty years old and was on the brink of a break down. I was going through a nasty divorce, and was trying to take care of my girls to make sure they were coping well. The truth is I was not coping at all. I was pushing everything aside and refusing to face the pain. It wasn't until my blood pressure sky rocketed, I had a major panic attack and I landed in hospital that I decided I was done putting my health at risk. I immediately went to see my general practitioner and crafted a plan to get back on track . It included healthy eating and working out. Most importantly, it included rest. Implementing this plan in my life was definitely a challenge, but beyond worth it. That is why I am so passionate about helping busy women learn about the importance of taking care of themselves. No matter how healthy you look or feel, you never know how much stress your body is truly carrying.

To be real with you, without your health, all of the other things you desire in life will not be easily obtained. Fitness is such an important investment into your health. The problem comes when we push it to the back burner for other commitments. While I am sure that the commitments you have are important, you cannot afford to push your fitness off either.

When I think of ways to make sure I am increasing my fitness habits, I have an acronym that assists me. It is F.I.T. This acronym stands for F- free your mind of what exercise should look like, I-incorporate exercise into your schedule, and T- talk to others about your desire. This acronym helps to remind me of the dedication I have made to my health.

The trouble is we have his idea of what being fit looks like. We assume it means you have to be skinny with muscles and no fat. Everyone's version of fit will look differently. You have to define what that looks like for you. For example, if someone ran track all their life, they may be able to begin running without an issue. Another person may have never run a day in their life, so they may begin their routine by walking. Neither is right or wrong. You have to make your fitness routine personal.

You can only be in shape by working on this. It must be something that is worked at on a regular basis. It cannot be something that just happens. Yes, it will be a challenge but it is something you can take steps towards.

The next step is to incorporate exercise into your schedule. For example, we plan out office meetings and our kids' extra-curricular activities, but we do not plan out our priorities. Make fitness a priority. Put this on your schedule in the same way you hold yourself accountable to go to an office meeting. When you schedule fitness, you are more likely to keep it. In order to add it to your schedule, you will want to get rid of something else. Take time to reflect on those things in your schedule that are sucking your time. Those time-suckers prevent us from being productive in things that have a far greater impact. I wrote a chapter on organizing your schedule, which will help your prioritize where your time should be spent.

You can exercise in increments, or you can exercise all at one time. It's up to you, but again you have to approach it in a way that works with your lifestyle. I have an exercise routine. During the weekdays I do three short 20-minute exercise segments. So for example, on a typical work day, I wake up and work out for 20 minutes and then I do a yoga DVD. On my lunch break, I often workout by walking for 20 minutes. Lastly, I follow up with a YouTube recording workout for 20 minutes. This happened in small segments, but I was still able to accomplish my goal of staying fit. On Friday evening and Saturday morning, since I have more time, I work out for one hour straight. This works for my schedule. You have to take time to reflect on your schedule and your needs. This will help you to determine the best approach to your schedule.

The last step would be to talk to others. When you let people know what you want to accomplish, it helps you to feel more accountable to follow though. Also, when you share this step in your life, you are able to be an example for others.

WAYS TO STAY ENCOURAGED:

1. Try different types of exercise (weight lifting, cardio, Zumba, yoga, etc.). Variety prevents you from becoming bored and complacent and then giving up.

2. Take it one step at a time. Small changes can have a big impact.

3. Involve your friends or family. When you involve others, it makes it fun and it's a great way to feel supported in your new change.

F. I. T.

F - Free your mind from what exercise "should" look like

I - Incorporate exercise into your schedule

T - Talk to others

REFLECTION

What is your biggest takeaway from this chapter?

_____

_____

_____

_____

What is one thing you can take off of your schedule to make room for exercise?

_____

_____

_____

_____

What is one strategy that you can use to make sure you stay F.I.T.?

_____

_____

_____

_____

CHAPTER 8: RELATIONSHIPS

"A good relationship creates an us without destroying me."

~Leo Buscaglia

$\mathcal{G}$rowing up, I always felt so different than my peers. I was driven and always had great ideas. The trouble I had is that I always shared all of the thoughts, and ideas with all of my friends. One time I shared the idea of creating a t shirt with one my friends and before I knew it. she was wearing and stealing my T-shirt design. This ate me alive not because she was wearing it, but because I felt betrayed. I remember speaking with my aunt who always gave me good advice; she told me I have to watch the relationships I have. She told me that people won't always mean well for me, and that part of life is learning who your real friends are.

That was one of the hardest lessons I learned. On that day, I recognized that people in your life are either adding and multiplying, or they are dividing and subtracting. You must take time to determine what those closest to you are doing, and removing those that are taking away from you and your success.

Having healthy relationships, whether they are business relationships, friendships, parenting or even intimate relationships, take work. A thriving, healthy relationship requires some give and take.

Like the quote says, good relationships should not make you have to change who you are to please someone else.

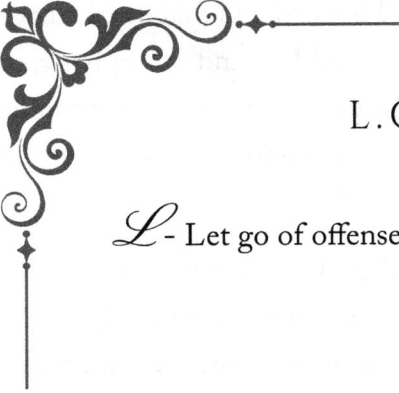

L.O.V.E.

L - Let go of offense

O - Open up and be vulnerable

V - View that person fairly

E - Encourage constant communication

Listed above is a great acronym I use to help ensure my relationships remain healthy and continue to grow. The truth is all relationships will have difficulties. There will be days where your spouse, child, parent, sibling or friend offends you. In order for a relationship to progress, you have to be willing to let go of offense. Honestly, when you hold on to what they did wrong and you play it in your mind over and over again, the only person you are hurting is yourself, and you are damaging the relationship. You know the old saying by Robin Sharma: "What you focus on grows." This is especially true when holding onto offense. When you remain offended, your level of anger, resentment, or frustration grows. You are no longer focusing on your relationship with the person. Instead, you are focused on a situation, and it keeps the relationship stagnant.

The second step is to be vulnerable. Vulnerability is often viewed as a sign of weakness when it is actually a sign of strength. Genuine vulnerability shows courage.

Vulnerability allows a relationship to be balanced. It lets the other person know what you need and it allows them to feel valuable. It also gives you a chance to trust them, and to be loved in return.

In friendships, vulnerability can mean you discuss a fear you have. In intimate relationships, vulnerability could be sharing a dream that you have never shared with anyone. In parenting, vulnerability could be admitting when you make mistakes. This allows your children to see that you too are human, but that you take responsibility for your choices. In a business setting, vulnerability could mean asking a trusted co-worker for support or help on a project. Vulnerability looks different in many different settings, but it is a key component to having healthy relationships.

The third key is to acknowledge that this person is human, and this means viewing them fairly. So many times as women, we get into relationships and set all of the expectations for those we care about. It is unfair for us to set these standards are expectations because we are all human and will never meet every single standard. When you go into a relationship understanding that the other person may fail, but that you care enough to accept them anyway—that is when the relationship becomes stronger.

The final step is the most important. In any successful relationship, communication should be a priority. Encouraging consistent communication can prevent misunderstandings which often lead to frustration, arguments, or even the severing of the relationship.

One thing that should be stressed is that listening is very important part of communication. You cannot expect to have positive communication if it is only one-sided. When listening, be sure you are engaged, focused, and dedicated to the other person's thoughts. If you are listening simply to prepare a response, you have not really listened.

We all know that everyone views situations differently. None of our realities are similar. This is important to remember when you are communicating with others. You do not have to always agree with everything they have said, but once you recognize that they are entitled to their own viewpoint from their own reality, you will be less likely to take different opinions personally.

Disclaimer: Take a moment to evaluate each relationship that you have. Is there value for both you and the other person in this relationship? These are tips to have healthy relationships. The key thing to remember is that it cannot be only one-sided. So if you have someone in your life who does not mean well, who constantly takes advantage of you, who is not genuinely dedicated to you or who puts in you in danger in any manner, these tips would not necessarily apply. because in that case you become a doormat. It is completely up to you, but I recommend that you remove anyone who no longer serves you. In relationships, people are either adding and multiplying to your life or they are subtracting and dividing. You want people who add value to your life, not take it away.

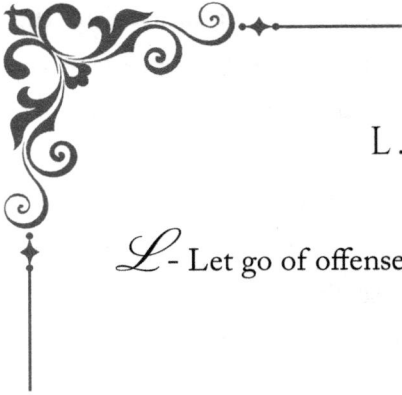

L.O.V.E

L - Let go of offense

O - Open up and be vulnerable

V - View that person fairly

E - Encourage constant communication

REFLECTION

What is your number one takeaway from this chapter?

_____

_____

_____

_____

What is the hardest part of being in a relationship with someone else? Why?

_____

_____

_____

_____

3. In what way can you implement the L.O.V.E. strategy into your business relationships, intimate relationships, parenting or friendships?

_____

_____

_____

_____

CHAPTER 9: SELF

"Invest in yourself; you can't afford not to."

~Nicolya Williams

I spent years trying to find myself. I tried to find myself based on society's standards, and I tried to define myself based on what other people said and believed about me. All these efforts were in vain because none of these things defined me. I learned that I had to define who I was and be confident in that opinion.

At the risk of being judged, I am going to honest. I lived in people bondage for years. I made choices based on what people told me to do, I made decisions based on what I thought people would think. The truth is I was not living my life for myself; Therefore I was miserable.

One of the best coaches I have ever had taught me about living for me and being happy within myself. I decided to take a risk and invest in myself. I stepped out of my comfort zone and in doing so it was the best experience ever. I learned that it is more difficult to try to live in a comfort zone than it is to follow your dreams, because the comfort zone is an illusion but your dreams are real. Once I started reaching my dreams and living them out, I realized how much time I had wasted living for other people and I vowed that I would not do that any more. This chapter is for women who want to be more of themselves and love every minute of it!

There is only one guaranteed investment in your life and that investment is yourself. The crazy part is that this is the least likely person we spend time investing in. It is so important that we learn to invest in ourselves. So many times we want to fix and change everything and everyone else around us, but we fail to recognize the improvements we should make within ourselves. Even small changes can have a large impact.

When people ask us to invest in them, we usually make a huge effort. Unfortunately, this makes us say no to ourselves. When we invest in ourselves, it is not considered selfish. When we invest in ourselves, we are able to make our life better, and those who are around us as well.

We often spend a good portion of our money and time on things such as cars, clothes, etc. True happiness comes from investing your money, time, and effort into the things that are important to you. New shoes and clothes might make you happy, but only temporarily.

These items are not valuable regardless of what society wants us to believe. BUT, you, my friend, are valuable. Therefore, the best investment will always be YOU! When you find time each day to invest in yourself, the payoff will be huge. You must make a better effort to learn that what you buy does not always have value, but when you invest in your personal development, you increase your value!

The best way to achieve a better quality of life to be successful, productive, and satisfied is to make it a point to invest in both personal and professional growth. The effort you put into consistently investing in yourself plays a large role in determining the quality of your life now and in the future. Some ways that you can invest in yourself are:

1. To explore your creative side. You have a creative side to you that has never fully been used. To say it boldly, you have yet to reach your creative potential. I spent years assuming I was not creative because I could not draw. Being creative is more than art. You can be creative by taking up a new hobby or learning a new language. This expands your thinking. Using your creative side allows you to face your life situations with a unique approach.

2. Develop your skills. There is more information than you can imagine on every single subject. Read books, articles, join an organization that inspires you, or attend a conference. Do the things that are related to the talent or skill you want to work on. The activities you participate in should add value and increase both your personal and professional development. They should not keep you stuck or stagnant.

3. Hire a coach. This is one of the most impactful decisions you can make in the process of your personal development. Think about it: do you expect yourself to fix the plumbing in your home? Or is it rational to assume that you are capable of teaching yourself German? So why is it that you expect that you will achieve your authentic and unique goals and desires in life just because? You see, the patterns and habits that you exhibit in life have made it challenging thus far in regards to you reaching your goals. With hiring a great coach, you will be able to set reasonable goals, you will be pushed to do things outside of your comfort zone and most importantly, you will be held accountable. Accountability is one thing that is practically impossible to do alone. So having the support from a coach increases the likelihood of follow through. In the words of Albert Einstein "Problems cannot be solved by the same level of thinking that created them". Therefore, you need to approach your problems differently. Coaches help you to gain clarity around the best approach, and enable you to get rid of the things that are not working. Hiring a life coach allows you to strengthen your personal foundation, raise your standards, eliminate tolerations and set boundaries. It also allows you to increase clarity about your purpose and what you want out of life. Coaching relationships are a powerful source of knowledge, motivation, inspiration and connections. They are the bridge from your dreams to making them a reality. Now it is up to you, to step out into your power and make it happen.

4. Practice Affirmations. Affirmations are an amazing way to allow your mind to focus on positive thoughts, and to work towards creating the reality you desire. The statements you make are aimed to positively impact your subconscious mind. Using affirmations helps you keep your mind focused on the goal you would like to accomplish, and it helps you stay positive and motivated. You would be surprised to see all that you can achieve simply by believing that the desire has already been fulfilled, and then affirming it.

Listed at the end of this chapter is an affirmation for each area of your life. These affirmations have been written to clear out the negative thoughts you may have about what you can receive in the various areas of your life. You may also feel free to write your own affirmations.

Say these affirmations out loud regularly, say them with love, faith, feeling and interest; feel and believe that your desire has already been fulfilled. When you believe this, you will accelerate its fulfillment. It is also helpful to visualize what each one of these affirmations will look like in your own personal life. This will inspire you to develop a habit of saying affirmations.

Doing the affirmations and visualization together allows for greater success. Know that it is never too late to be what you might have been, and start affirming what you want into your life. So, clear your mind and allow your life to align with your goals, because they can come true...you just have to believe!

Thoughts - I think positive thoughts with ease.

Habits - I practice beneficial and positive habits daily.

Goals - My potential to succeed is limitless.

Schedule - I have a well-balanced life.

Home - I make daily choices to create a harmonious environment for myself and those whom I love.

Finances - I am willing, ready and able to receive money.

Health - My body is healthy, I am wealthy and my mind is wise.

Relationships - My relationships are becoming stronger, deeper and more stable each day.

Self - I am confident and I believe in myself.

CHAPTER 10:
MAINTAINING MOMENTUM

"Motivation is what get's you started and habit is what keeps you going"

~Jim Ryun

I want to congratulate you on taking the powerful step. Implementing the skills in this book will allow you to live a well disciplined and planned out life. I am not by any means promising that every day will run smooth, but you now have a plan to help tackle those obstacles. You will no longer be controlled by overwhelm or uncertainty.

Many women confuse being busy with being productive. There is a major difference amongst the two. Busy women are consistently doing something, but typically have nothing to show for it. They try to balance everything, but often feel out of alignment or overwhelmed. Productive people are focused on the most important tasks, and make completion a priority. They also prioritize the things that they are working on. My hope is that you have already started to make progress in changing your mentality about being busy. Going forward you will want to measure your progress and performance to ensure that you are still implementing these tips effectively. Here are six questions that you should reflect on daily to ensure that you are being productive instead of just being busy.

- Did I have a positive attitude today?

- Did I make healthy choices today in regards to my rest, exercise, and food? How was my energy?

- Are my habits in alignment with what I wanted to accomplish today?

- Have I nurtured the relationships that I value?

- Did I make the best use of my time?

- Did I make time for myself today?

Quick Tips for Busy Women was created for you to make major shifts in your life to live the way that you desire. Do not make the mistake of reading this book and walking away. You only have one life to live, and it is important to live it in a way that makes you happy. Therefore you must make a non-negotiable decision to implement the tips outlined in this book. Majority of women will read personal development books, and self-help books. While reading these books they feel inspired, but refuse to implement anything. They then go on and live the way that they have been living. Do NOT become a statistic. Don't read this book and walk away, refusing to take action on any of the tips here. Life won't change unless you make changes.

Use what you learned from this book, apply it daily, and be patient as you learn. Nothing changes unless you change it, so you have to make those shifts. It is well known that the definition of insanity is to keep doing the same things over and over but expecting a different result. You have to make changes and you have to make them now. It is easy to push these things aside or to feel like it won't work for you. As tempting as that is, I want to remind you that in order to make progress,the key is to be disciplined and consistent for an extended period of time. The level of your consistency and discipline will truly determine your outcome.

Until the pain of staying the same becomes greater than the pain of change, everything will remain the way it is. But you are different; you picked up this book because you were ready for change. Change is not the result of a miracle. It is the outcome of hard work and dedication. In order to have change, you must be open to your personal growth. Yes, change is uncomfortable and it is also hard. But, anything that is truly of value or worth it takes hard work, and you must be dedicated to the process. It is the only way. You must believe that you are stronger than any pattern, habit or situation, because you are. It is possible for you to live a balanced life, and it will happen with hard work, planning, focused energy, and dedication.

Take this information and make a plan for your next steps. In my next book *The Devoted Dreamers*, I talk about how important it is to not only have a daily routine and plan for success, but also to have an evening ritual that helps you plan for your next day. When you go to sleep with a plan you will wake up with a purpose! Step outside of your comfort zone, because nothing good comes from it. Become over-committed to reaching your potential, that's where the real magic lies. If you walk away from this book without implementing what you have learned, do not be surprised if your life remains the same. I mean, after all, the definition of insanity is doing the same thing over again, but expecting a different result. It is time for a change, it is time for you to approach life differently if you want different results! Now is not the time to doubt yourself or review all of your fears. Now is the time to take what you learned and push harder than you could ever imagine. Your future self will indeed thank you!

Quick Tips For Busy Women Workbook

By: Nicolya Williams

The Quick Tips for Busy Women Workbook was created for women like you to make MAJOR shifts in their lives. Use this time as an opportunity to reflect on the various areas of your life and how you can make improvements. This book will help you to cultivate a more positive approach to the various areas in your life.

Mindset

How do you feel about your goals?

_____

_____

_____

_____

What negative thoughts interfere with this?

_____

_____

_____

_____

How can you challenge those thoughts?

_____

_____

_____

_____

What are ways to FREE your thoughts?

_____

_____

_____

_____

Habits

What are your daily habits?

_____

_____

_____

_____

How do these habits align with your goals?

_____

_____

_____

_____

How are they serving you?

_____

_____

_____

_____

In what ways are they negatively impacting you?

_____

_____

_____

_____

Why do you think it is time to change them?

_____

_____

_____

_____

Goals

What are your goals?

_____

_____

_____

_____

What are your thoughts, feelings and beliefs about your goals?

_____

_____

_____

_____

How do you know that this goal is unique to you?

_____

_____

_____

_____

Schedule

What is your schedule like?

_____

_____

_____

_____

How do you know which things are a priority?

_____

_____

_____

_____

What do you do to prepare yourself each night and each morning?

_____

_____

_____

_____

What areas in your schedule need to be changed?

_____

_____

_____

Home

What does your home say about you?

_____

_____

_____

_____

What areas in your home do you like?

_____

_____

_____

_____

What areas in your home do you dislike?

_____

_____

_____

_____

Finances

Reflect on your budget.

_____

_____

_____

_____

What is going well with your budget?

_____

_____

_____

_____

What should be changed?

_____

_____

_____

_____

When looking at your last 15 purchases what does that say about your life,
values and priorities?

Health

What do you do each day that contributes positively to your health?

_____

_____

_____

_____

What do you need to change?

_____

_____

_____

_____

When reflecting on your health now how do you feel about it?

_____

_____

_____

_____

How can you be F.I.T.?

_____

_____

_____

_____

Relationships

How do you feel about all of your relationships?

_____

_____

_____

_____

Are they healthy?

_____

_____

_____

_____

Are they adding to your life?

_____

_____

_____

_____

How can you make L. O. V.E. apply to your life?

_____

_____

_____

_____

Self Care

What is your self care life like?

_____

_____

_____

_____

Do you make regular time for yourself?

_____

_____

_____

_____

What are some activities that you enjoy doing?

_____

_____

_____

_____

What are some ways that you can increase your self care?

_____

_____

_____

_____

NICOLYA WILLIAMS is a certified life coach and blogger for women. She is also licensed as a clinical counselor and worked in her field for several years. As a coach, she divides her time between empowering women one on one, and motivating groups of women through master classes. When not spending time on her business, Nicolya enjoys spending time with family, reading, attending church, or exercising at the gym. Nicolya resides in a suburb of Columbus, Ohio with her two daughters.

Nicolya has a Masters of Science in Education, MSE., and holds certifications as a Certified Coach Practitioner, CCP., Licensed Professional Counselor, LPC., Licensed Professional School Counselor, LPSC., and a Chemical Dependency Counselor Assistant, CDCA.

You can connect with Nicolya at www.nicolyawilliams.com or on social media platforms @NicolyaWilliams

Clarity Cove Publishing

We publish books the world needs

Clarity Cove Publishing was created by Nicolya Williams. Clarity Cove Publishing connects with powerful, determined and driven women to help them turn their message into their masterpiece. We offer publishing services, writing assistance, marketing strategies and much more. Our vision is to foster creativity, encourage risk taking and increase clarity around your book writing goals. Our authors have an opportunity to get their message out into the masses without losing their authenticity in the process.

To inquire about publishing with us or getting support along your publishing journey, reach out to us at

http://www.nicolyawilliams.com/clarity-cove-publishing/

or email

claritycove@nicolyawilliams.com

www.ingramcontent.com/pod-product-compliance
Lightning Source LLC
Chambersburg PA
CBHW071602040426
42452CB00008B/1259